POPULAR SAX SOLOS

Editor's Note:

Chord names in italics reflect actual sounding chords.
Chord names in regular type reflect chords respective to sax's written key.

Transcribed by John Nicholas

Cherry Lane Music Company
Director of Publications/Project Editor: Mark Phillips

ISBN 978-1-60378-431-3

Visit our website at www.cherrylaneprint.com

CONTENTS

After the Love Has Gone

Alto Sax
3:42

Words and Music by David Foster,
Jay Graydon and Bill Champlin

Slowly, in 2

All the Way from Memphis

Tenor Sax

2:08

Words and Music by Ian Hunter

Moderately fast

Arthur's Theme

(Best That You Can Do)
from ARTHUR an ORION PICTURES release through WARNER BROS.

Words and Music by
Burt Bacharach, Carole Bayer Sager,
Christopher Cross and Peter Allen

Bad to the Bone

Alto Sax

Words and Music by George Thorogood

Badlands

Words and Music by Bruce Springsteen

Baker Street

Alto Sax

0:25

Words and Music by Gerry Rafferty

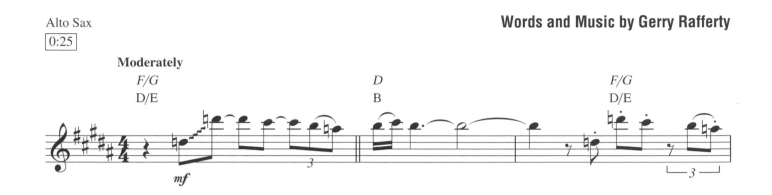

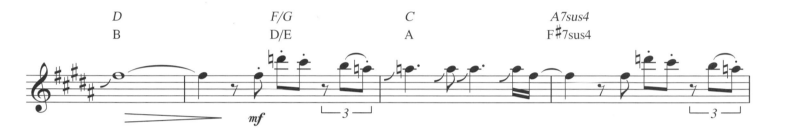

Born to Run

**Words and Music by
Bruce Springsteen**

Tenor Sax

1:53

Fast Rock

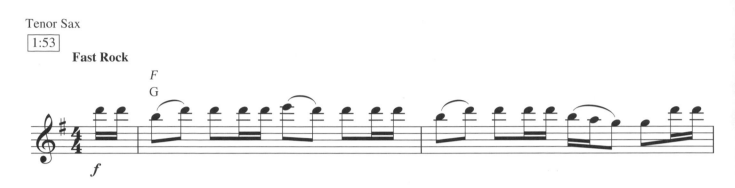

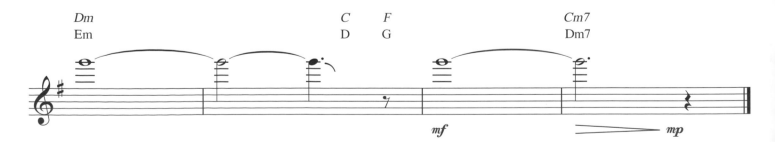

Brown Sugar

Tenor Sax

Words and Music by
Mick Jagger and Keith Richards

1:39

Moderately fast

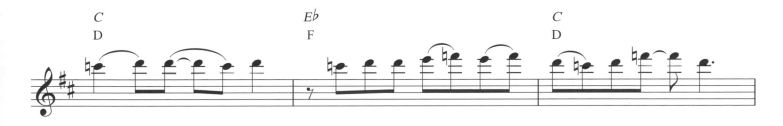

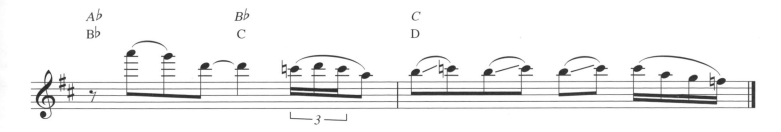

Careless Whisper

Words and Music by
George Michael and Andrew Ridgeley

Alto Sax

0:01

Moderately

Cut the Cake

Alto Sax

Written by James Stuart,
Alan Gorrie, Roger Ball
and Owen Mcintyre

13

Dancing in the Dark

**Words and Music by
Bruce Springsteen**

Tenor Sax

3:24

Freeway of Love

Words and Music by
Narada Michael Walden
and Jeffrey Cohen

Doctor Wu

**Words and Music by
Walter Becker and Donald Fagen**

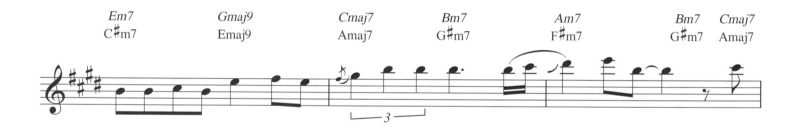

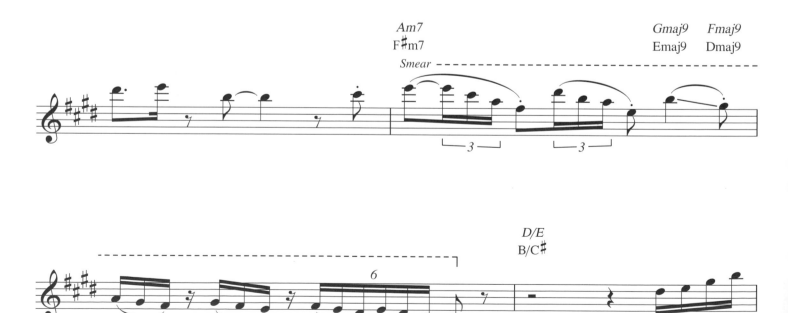

I Can't Go for That

Words and Music by
**Daryl Hall, John Oates
and Sara Allen**

Alto Sax

2:42

Moderately

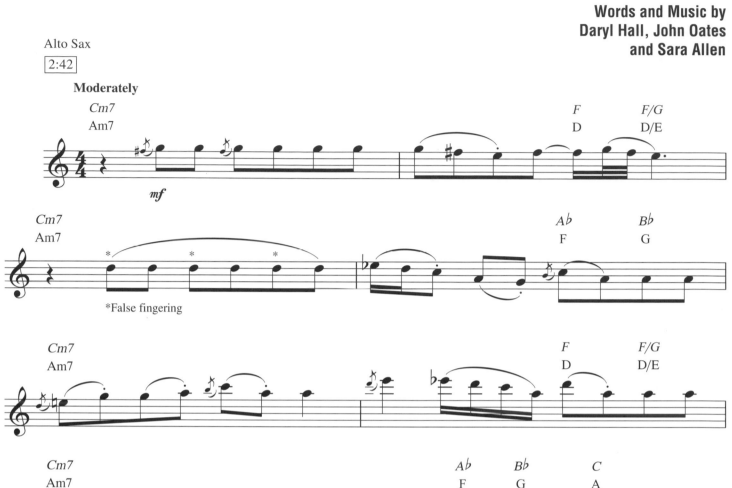

*False fingering

I Missed Again

Words and Music by
Phil Collins

Tenor Sax

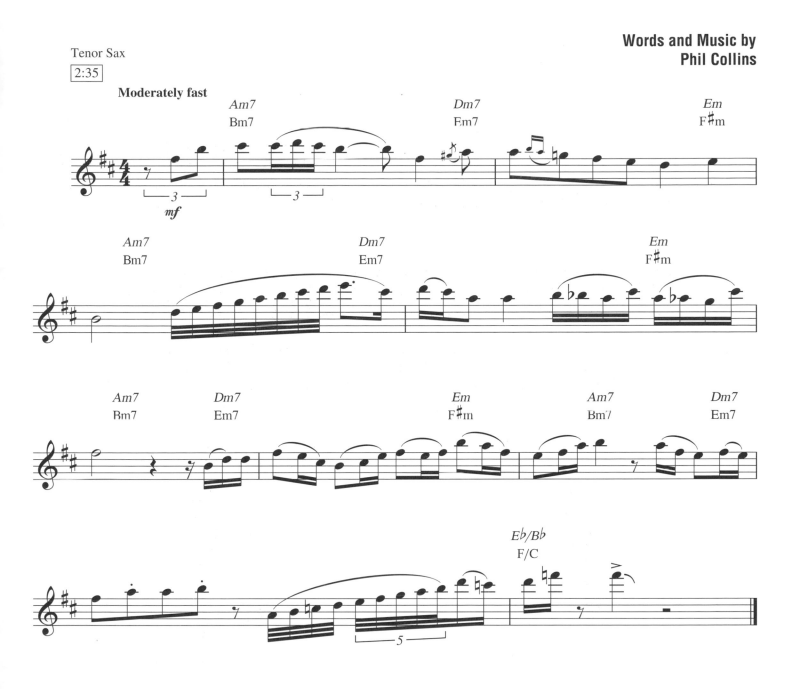

I Wanna Be Loved

**Words and Music by
Farnell Jenkins**

Tenor Sax

2:05

Moderately

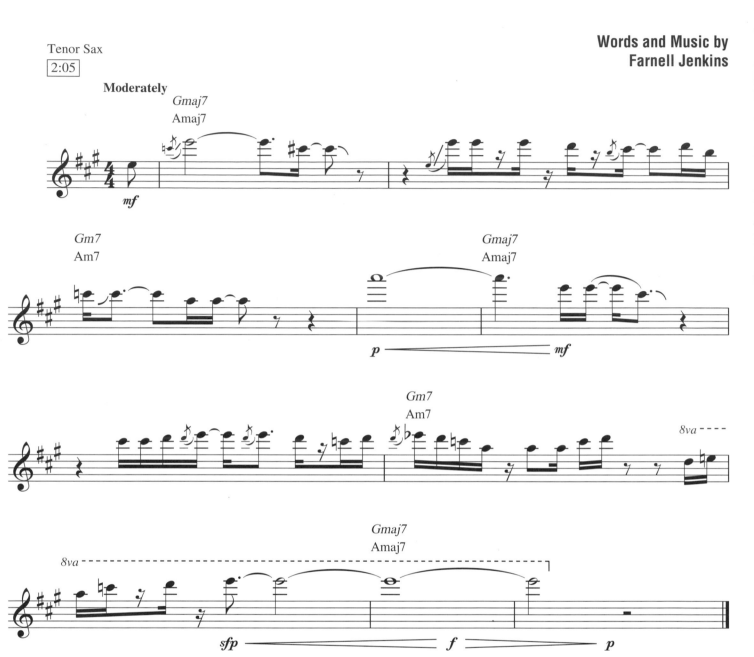

It's Still Rock and Roll to Me

**Words and Music by
Billy Joel**

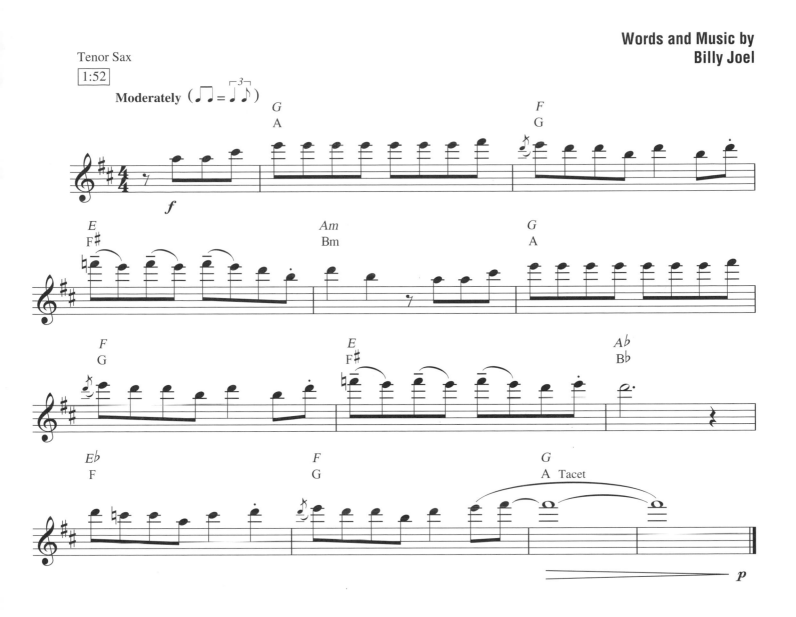

Jazzman

Words and Music by
Carole King and David Palmer

Alto Sax

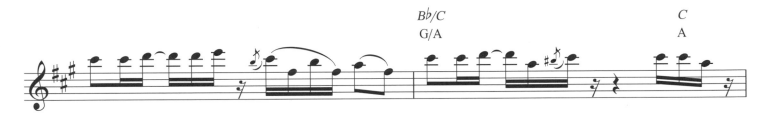

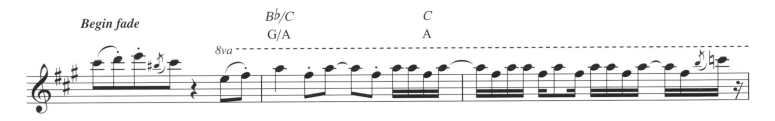

Modern Love

Words and Music by
David Bowie

Baritone Sax

1:57

Fast Rock

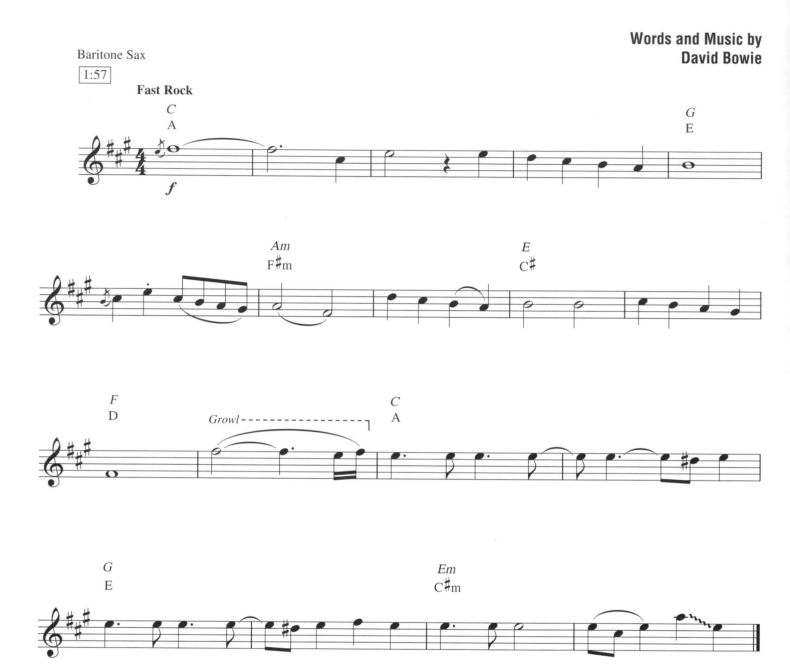

Moonlighting

Words by Al Jarreau
Music by Lee Holdridge

Music

Words and Music by
Carole King

New York State of Mind

Tenor Sax

Words and Music by
Billy Joel

Old Time Rock & Roll

Words and Music by
George Jackson
and Thomas E. Jones III

Tenor Sax

1:55

Moderately

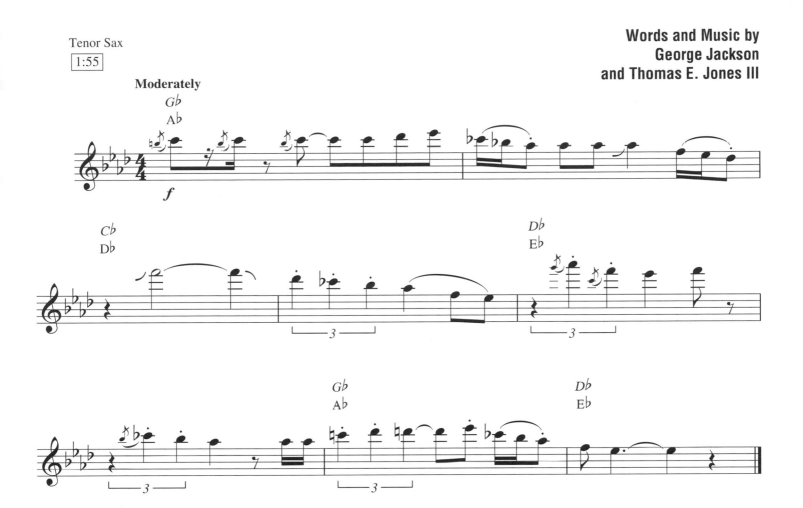

One More Night

Words and Music by
Phil Collins

Alto Sax

3:47

Moderately slow, in 2

One Year of Love

Alto Sax

Words and Music by
John Deacon

Roll with It

Words and Music by
**Will Jennings, Steve Winwood,
Eddie Holland, Lamont Dozier
and Brian Holland**

Tenor Sax

2:17

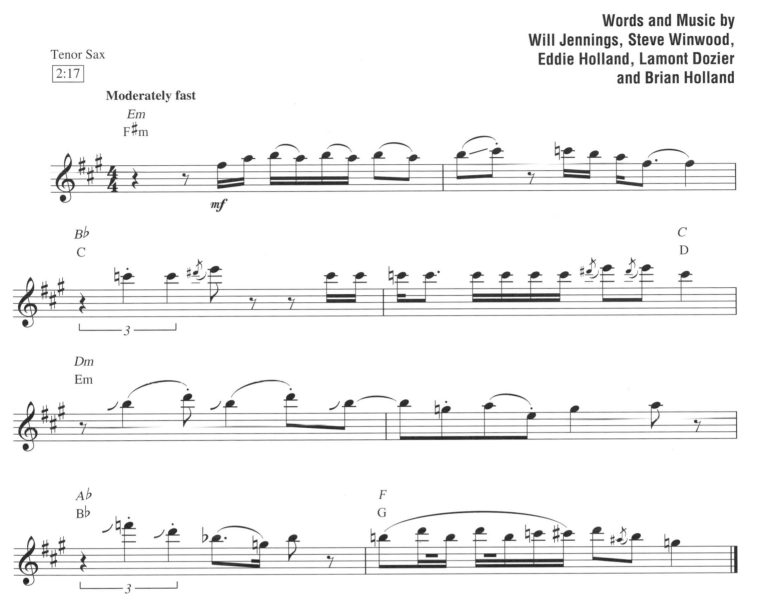

Same Old Song and Dance

Tenor Sax

Words and Music by
Steven Tyler and Joe Perry

Say Goodbye to Hollywood

Words and Music by
Billy Joel

Tenor Sax

She's Gone

Words and Music by
Daryl Hall and John Oates

Soprano Sax

2:54

Moderately

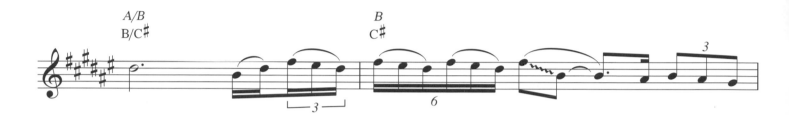

Waiting on a Friend

**Words and Music by
Mick Jagger and Keith Richards**

Tenor Sax

1:54

Moderately

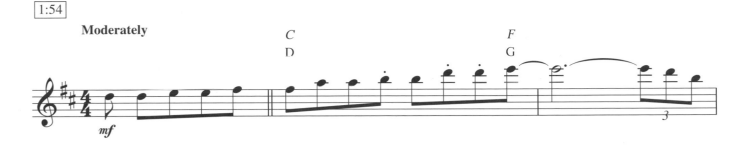

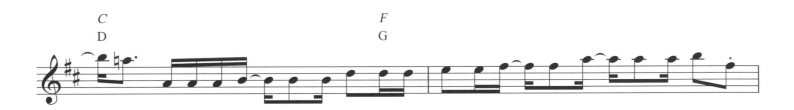

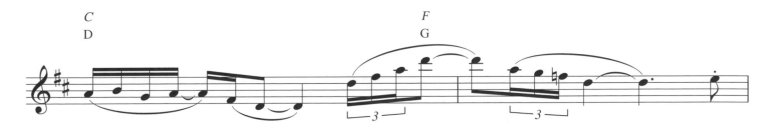

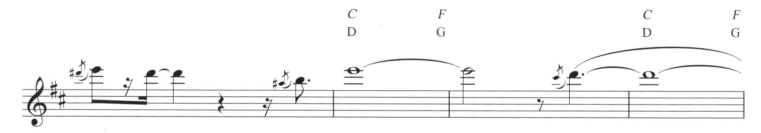

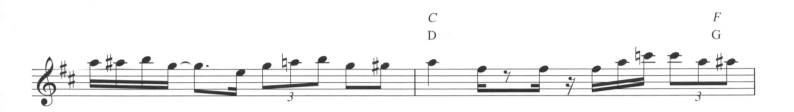

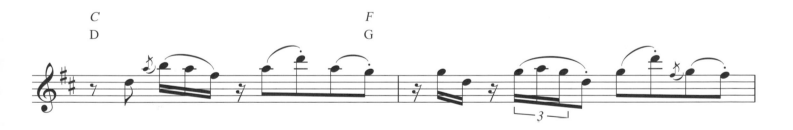

Begin fade

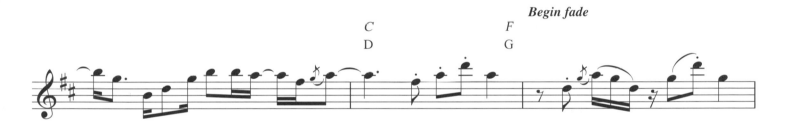

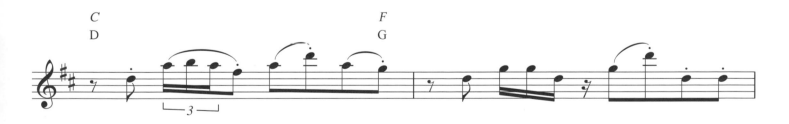

Fade out

Smooth Operator

Words and Music by
Helen Adu and Ray St. John

Tenor Sax

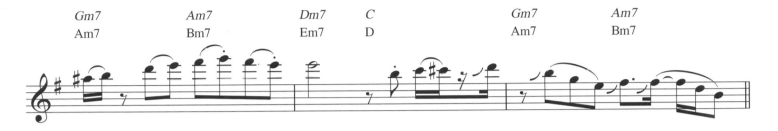

3:54

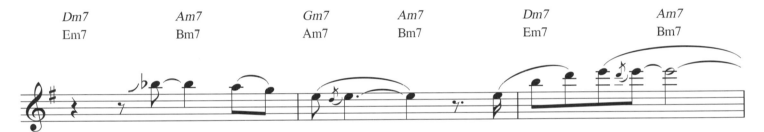

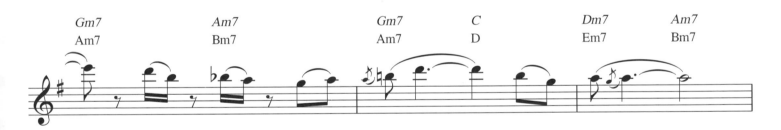

Begin fade

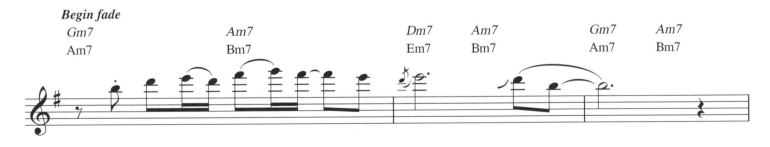

Fade out

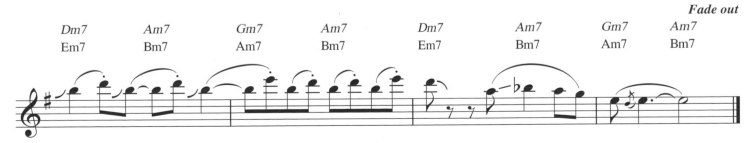

Us and Them

Words by Roger Waters
Music by Roger Waters and Rick Wright

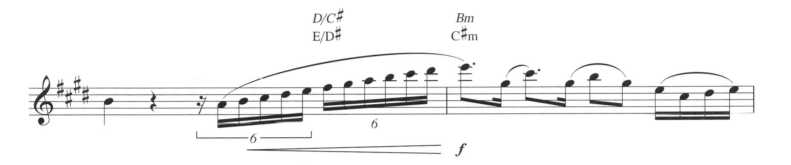

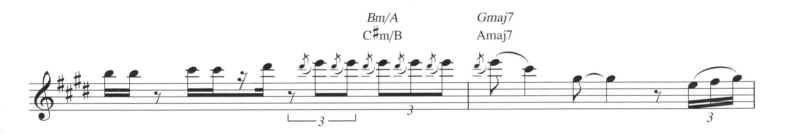

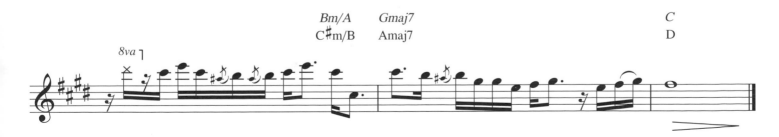

Who Can It Be Now?

Tenor Sax

Words and Music by
Colin Hay

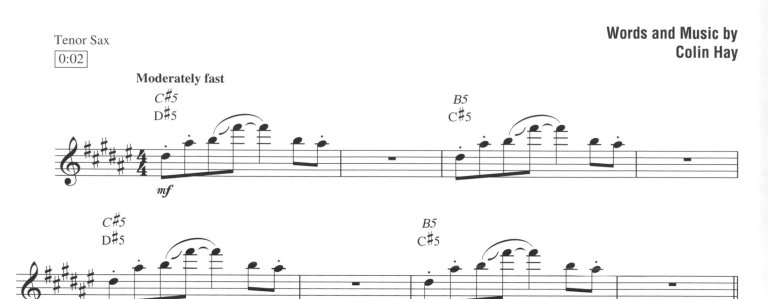

Young Americans

Alto Sax

Words and Music by
David Bowie

Will You

Words and Music by
Hazel O'Connor and Wesley Magoogan

48

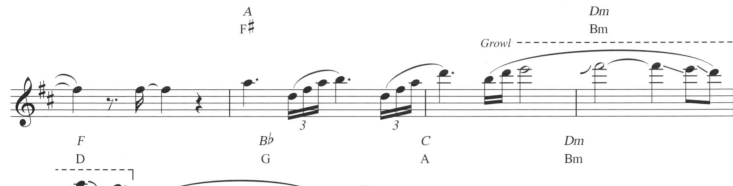

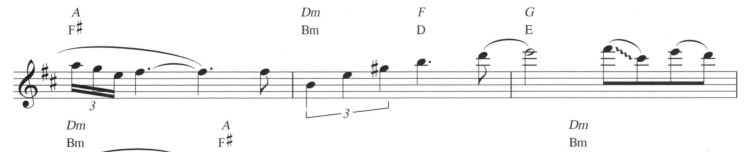

Year of the Cat

Words and Music by
Ian Alastir Stewart and Peter Wood

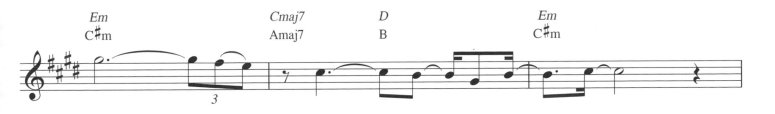

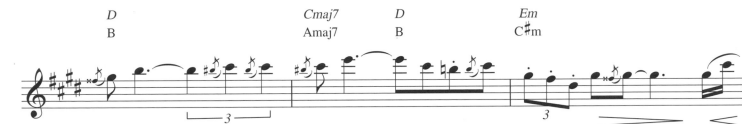

Begin fade

Fade out

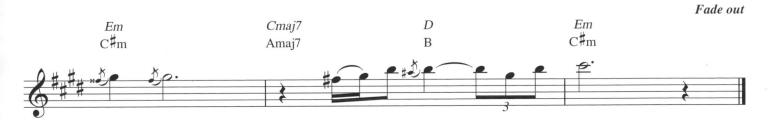

You Belong to the City

Words and Music by
Glenn Frey and Jack Tempchin

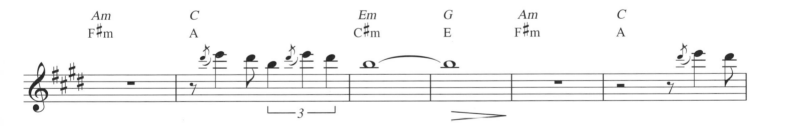

Your Latest Trick

Words and Music by
Mark Knopfler

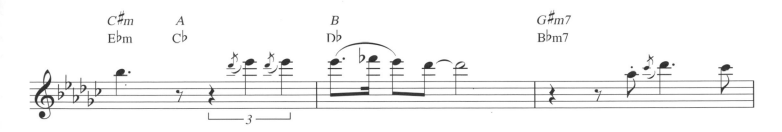

Begin fade

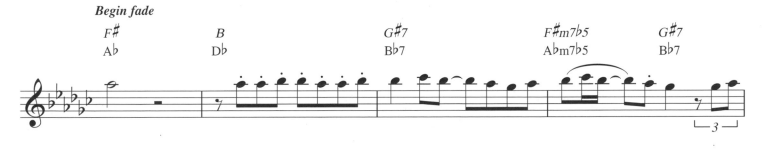

Fade out

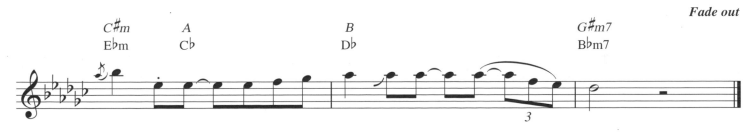

Young Blood

**Words and Music by
Rickie Lee Jones**

Soprano Sax

3:21

Moderately

*Soprano overdub.

Begin fade

Fade out